ORANGUTAN
HATS and Other Tools Animals Use

Richard Haynes

illustrated by **Stephanie Laberis**

CANDLEWICK PRESS

CONTENTS

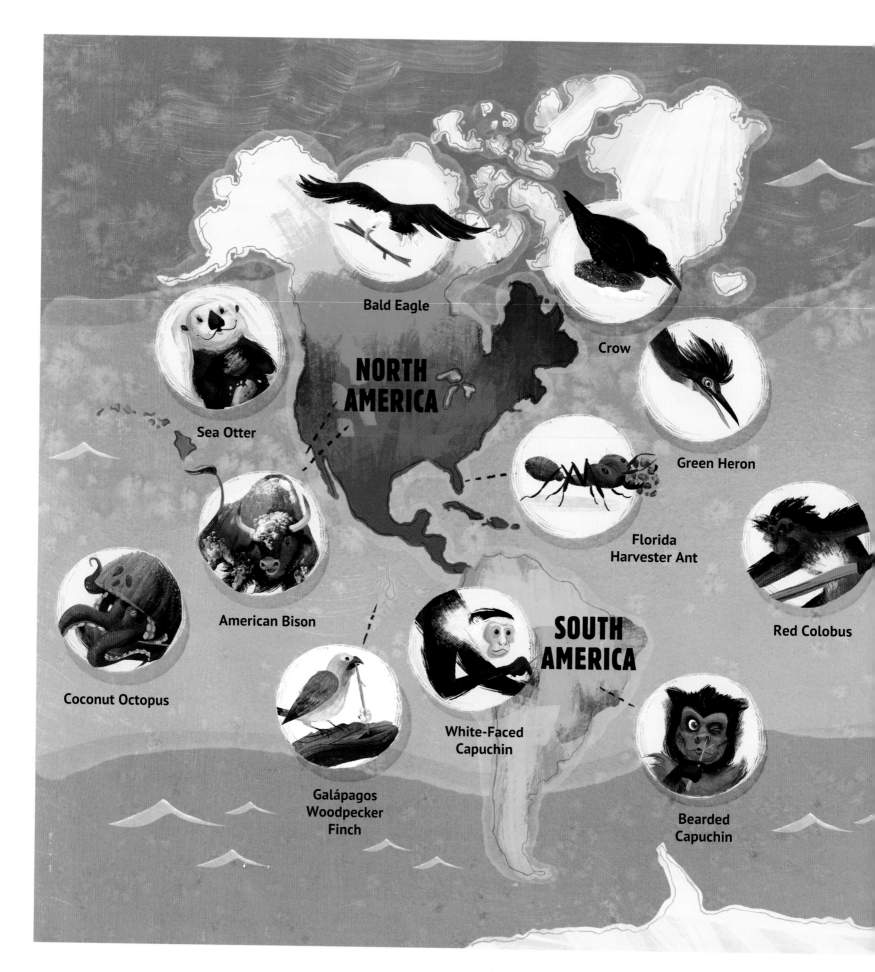

Bald Eagle

Crow

NORTH AMERICA

Sea Otter

Green Heron

Florida Harvester Ant

American Bison

White-Faced Capuchin

SOUTH AMERICA

Red Colobus

Coconut Octopus

Galápagos Woodpecker Finch

Bearded Capuchin

White Stork

ASIA

EUROPE

Olive
Baboon

Long-Tailed
Tailorbird

Long-Tailed
Macaque

AFRICA

Orangutan

Black-and-White
Colobus

AUSTRALIA

African
Elephant

Bottlenose Dolphin

Boxer Crab

INTRODUCTION

What Is a Tool?

For as long as humans have searched for food, water, shelter, safety, comfort, health, recreation, or peace of mind, they have used tools to help achieve these goals. A tool is any functional object, fashioned or found, that is not a part of the user.

A tool can be as simple as a wheel or as complex as an engine. Wheels can help transport everyday loads great and small, while fuel-injected rocket engines can send a spaceship to the moon and back. Tools can help with everything from homework to hygiene. A toothbrush is a tool. A pencil and ruler are tools. A tool can help with cracking a nut or catching a fish.

For thousands of years, it was believed that only humans were intelligent enough to invent and use tools. Charles Darwin, in *The Descent of Man* (1871), challenged this long-held notion by pointing out tool use in primates. Since 1960, the observations of biologists, zoologists, and other animal behavior specialists, including the groundbreaking study of chimpanzees in Tanzania, Africa, by renowned primatologist Jane Goodall, have provided more recent eye-opening research. These studies have shown that other animals besides humans can puzzle out ways to use and adapt common objects to assist in their daily quest for survival.

From orangutans to Galápagos woodpecker finches, from boxer crabs to Florida harvester ants, all sorts of animals around the globe use tools in astonishing ways!

TOOLS FOR STAYING NEAT AND CLEAN

Animals groom themselves for the same reasons we do: to keep neat, clean, and healthy. Dirty skin and hair are more likely to attract flies and bugs, which can carry disease. To stay ahead of dirt and disease, some animals have discovered that tools can be of help.

Napkins

Ripe, juicy fruit is a large part of the diet of orangutans in Borneo and chimpanzees in Africa, but it can be messy. Unless the animals clean themselves up, the juice that gets on their hands, face, and fur can attract insects. Bugs would happily burrow down into the primates' fur or skin, causing irritation or, worse, disease. So orangutans and chimpanzees grab a leaf from a nearby bush or tree and use this natural napkin to wipe themselves down and clean up the mess.

Toilet Paper

Orangutans, bonobos, and chimpanzees use leaves not just as napkins but as toilet paper, too.

Toothbrush

After a meal of sticky fruit, orangutans give their teeth a scrub by chewing on a mouthful of leaves, then spitting them out.

Nose Picker

Booger alert! Bearded capuchin monkeys from Brazil use sticks or pieces of grass to clean their noses.

Floss

The long-tailed macaque doesn't like to have anything caught between its teeth—not even a tiny seed or shred of coconut. The trapped piece of food can be uncomfortable. Also, if it isn't removed, it will rot, causing cavities and tooth decay over time. To dig out those pieces stuck between its teeth, a macaque uses twigs, long coconut fibers, or even pieces of its own hair to dislodge the food.

Female macaques floss slowly in order to show their young how it's done. *Up, down, up, down*—and out flies a seed or a little chunk of food.

Visitors to a Buddhist shrine in Thailand supply the macaques that gather there with a particularly nice source of floss: a monkey occasionally boldly jumps onto a person's back and steals a strand of hair, plucking it right off the worshipper's head! Because the temple macaques are so revered, people good-naturedly tolerate the hair pulling.

TOOLS FOR HEALTH AND HEALING

Distress or injury can cause animals to weaken and leave them open to life-threatening danger from predators. To stay as healthy as possible, a few animals have developed ingenious ways to heal themselves.

Sunscreen

Standing out in the hot sun for hours can start to burn even an elephant's tough, leathery skin. To prevent painful sunburn, elephants make their own sunscreen. First, the elephant wets its skin by taking a bath in a muddy wallow or pool of water. Then, using its trunk, it tosses up clumps of dust, which stick to its damp skin. This paste becomes sunscreen. No dust? The elephant will grab straw, grass, mud, or even throw-up to coat its skin instead. An elephant would rather be covered in vomit than in blisters!

Tick Removal

Picture a tiny tick on the leg of a massive elephant. Seems like the bigger creature would have the advantage, right? The mighty elephant goes after the bloodsucker with its strong and flexible trunk. It nudges and pushes. No luck! The tick already has its barbed hypostome, or mouthpiece, deep into the elephant's skin. Holding a slender stick in its trunk, the elephant goes after that tick again, prying, prodding, and poking until it finally manages to dislodge the tick or crush it dead.

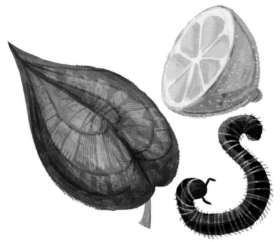

Insect Repellent

To keep biting bugs away, spider monkeys rub themselves with either lime juice or crushed ants and millipedes, whose bodies contain acids and other chemicals that work as a natural insect repellent.

White-faced capuchins of Costa Rica rub themselves with the leaves of certain kinds of pepper plants, the oils of which are a natural insect repellent.

Antiseptic

The pepper-plant leaves are also antiseptic, which means they have properties that slow or prevent the growth of bacteria and other germs that can cause infection.

Pain Relief

When an orangutan's muscles are sore, it chews up a bunch of leaves from a plant called *Dracaena cantleyi*, which scientists discovered have anti-inflammatory properties, meaning they can help reduce swelling. The orangutan applies the gooey green paste of the leaves and its own saliva to the places that ache. Relief!

Burn Cream

Following a forest fire in Kapuas, Central Kalimantan, in Borneo, an observant rescuer noticed that the orangutans were applying the sap of the pantung tree to the soles of their hands and feet. Just as *Dracaena cantleyi* leaves can soothe sore muscles, pantung sap can offer relief from painful burns.

TOOLS FOR DEFENSE

The best tool users in the wild, when it comes to protecting themselves, are monkeys and larger apes, such as the olive baboon. They throw branches, rocks, or even fruit if they feel threatened. Most animals in the wild have a few basic strategies for avoiding or fending off predators: run, hide, or fight. Some, however, have additional tricks for staying alive, using—what else?—tools!

Weapons

If a chick falls out of its nest before it is fledged, it becomes easy prey. To protect its fallen chick, an American crow might caw and make a racket to distract or scare away a predator. If that doesn't work, the crow will drop sticks, pinecones, and even rocks onto any creature that gets too close.

It's no secret that a skunk sprays a nasty-smelling liquid when it feels threatened. Likewise, the Australian brush turkey uses a weapon of its own. When pursued by its predator the lace monitor lizard, a brush turkey kicks back some sand, gravel, or loose earth, aiming for the attacker's face. An eyeful of grit will stop the lizard in its tracks.

If a turtle gets too close to a fish that a bald eagle has its eye on, the eagle may snatch a stick in its beak and use it to whack the turtle. This is a surefire way to get the turtle's attention and scare it off. Beat it!

From Africa to South America, monkeys and apes have been known to use sticks to beat venomous snakes to death or to free themselves from the grip of a powerful python. Primates have also been known to use a stick as a club or spear against lions.

11

Shields

To look bigger and scarier, a tiny boxer crab will pick up and carry around a small anemone in each of its two front claws. (That's how it got the nicknames of pom-pom crab and cheerleader crab.) The threat of a deadly sting from the anemones' tentacles scares away the boxer crab's predators like the goby fish. But the crab must be equally wary of the anemones' paralyzing poison sting.

Some hermit crabs use stinging anemones for protection from fish and octopuses by placing an anemone on the back of its shell, or in the opening of its shell after it withdraws safely inside.

Deception

When danger nears, orangutans and chimpanzees will "snag crash" or "thump." An orangutan will push a dead tree over with a loud crash. *Timber!* A chimpanzee will pick up a large log and slam it to the ground—*ka-thump!* Both techniques give the impression of a much mightier creature on the move, thus alarming and discouraging the advancing predator.

Even a simple blade of grass can turn into an effective tool of defensive deception. An orangutan holds a piece of grass up to its mouth and, blowing hard, makes a loud and unfamiliar noise. Called kiss-squeaking, this sudden, shrill chirp coming from the jungle canopy echoes in and around the treetops, giving a surround-sound sense of danger, and is a good trick for alarming and frightening off a potential attacker.

The Pacific and Indian Oceans are home to the veined or coconut octopus. This intelligent cephalopod has found a unique tool for protecting itself from predators like viperfish, great white sharks, and larger octopuses.

Countless empty coconut shells litter the bottom of these tropical oceans. The veined octopus uses the shells like stilts to make itself look taller, bigger, and more imposing. If a hungry fish gets too close, the octopus can also curl into a tight ball, tuck itself into the shells, and pull the two halves together tightly.

To further fool predators, the octopus can even make the coconut roll, as if it is just an ordinary coconut being swept along by the motion of the ocean.

Diplomacy

Who's in charge? Animals of a single species will fight, claw, scratch, bite, and butt heads just to decide which one of them is boss. The western red colobus monkey, whose home range is found in forests from Senegal to Ghana, in West Africa, has developed a more peaceful way to settle this issue. An adult male grabs one end of a long stick and takes it to a rival adult male. If the rival accepts the challenge, he takes hold of the opposite end of the stick and the two have an old-fashioned tug-of-war. The outcome of the match will settle the matter of dominance simply and without bloodshed.

TOOLS FOR HUNTING, HARVESTING, AND EATING

When it comes to finding food and water, animals have figured out creative ways of getting the job done.

Hammers and Anvils

The Egyptian vulture, found in parts of Africa, Europe, and India, has a taste for ostrich eggs. The black-breasted buzzard of Australia has a similar taste for emu eggs. But the curved beaks of these scavengers are not built for breaking open eggshells. Their beaks are better adapted for tearing meat from carcasses. Both birds have figured out that dropping a rock onto the egg—from close by or overhead—can help. It may take a few tries, but eventually the weight of the rock and gravity combine to crack the shell open. Then the hungry bird swoops down and sucks up a high-protein meal.

Because the waters they live in are so cold—between thirty and sixty degrees Fahrenheit—sea otters burn energy quickly. They need lots of calories to keep warm—25 percent of their body weight every day, in fact. No wonder sea otters spend so much time searching for food. Their diet is made up of abalones, crabs, sea urchins, clams, mussels, and snails, many of which have shells that are tough to pry open. Abalones cling so tightly to rocks, they're hard to pry loose.

To get at its lunch, a sea otter uses a rock like a hammer, knocking an abalone loose. Or it uses two rocks like a hammer and anvil. The otter floats on its back in a bed of sea kelp, rests one rock on its chest, places a shellfish on that rock, and uses another rock to strike at the shell. Caught between a rock and a hard place, the shell is cracked open. Lunch is served.

Shovels

Bearded capuchin monkeys rely on tubers as a food source. But the ground can be rock-hard during the dry season, making it impossible to get at tubers using only their hands. These skillful monkeys use fist-size stones to pound away at and pulverize the hard soil with rapid strikes, scooping out the loosened dirt as they go. Their efforts eventually uncover fat, juicy, potato-like tubers. Now they can settle down for some good munching and crunching.

Bait and Lures

The green heron of North, Central, and South America stands motionless, waiting for fish to swim by. But if fish don't swim close enough to the shoreline, what's a heron to do?

Herons have observed that fish like to eat insects and earthworms. The green heron has learned how to bait and set a trap to lure a fish closer. The heron finds a tasty morsel and drops it into the water nearby. Along comes a fish, ready for a snack, and—*snap!*— the unsuspecting fish *is* the snack.

Termites are neat freaks and take swift action whenever any member of the colony dies, removing carcasses from the mound immediately. This is insurance against diseases that could wipe out the entire colony. The neotropical assassin bug takes full advantage of this habit by waving the carcass of a termite over the opening to a colony.

When a member of the termite cleanup crew emerges and takes hold of the carcass, the assassin bug slowly draws the baited body out, then eats the live termite. The assassin bug will repeat this trick seven or eight times in a row. Termites fall for it again and again. *Tasty termite treats!*

The burrowing owl's diet is bugs and beetles, even dung beetles. The dung beetle's diet is—you guessed it—poop! To lure its dinner, the owl will scatter pellets of other animal dung around the entrance of its burrow. Along comes an unsuspecting dung beetle looking for a nutritious pile of poop. In one quick strike, the dung beetle is gone and the owl's appetite is satisfied.

Mugger crocodiles and American alligators are sneaky-smart when it comes to luring their prey. These big-toothed, snappy-jawed reptiles collect sticks that are the same size and shape as the sticks herons and egrets favor for building nests. Once they've built up an attractive floating mound of nest-building materials, the reptiles duck under the deadly trap. Enticed by the ready supply of perfect sticks, a nest-building bird swoops down to pick one up and . . . *chomp* . . . the bird is gone in one bite, feathers and all.

Probes

Colobuses (black-and-white ones as well as red ones), mangabeys, olive baboons, lion-tailed macaques, chimpanzees, and orangutans have all been observed in the wild using sticks either as poking and probing tools or as shovels. Monkeys and apes shove a stick into a termite or ant nest, then wait until a watchful ant or termite attacks and sinks their jaws into the "intruder." When the monkey or ape pulls out the stick, instant insect kebab!

Hooks

The Galápagos woodpecker finch from Santa Cruz Island in the Galápagos uses thorny twigs from blackberry bushes to hook and pull grubs and larvae from under the bark of *Scalesia* trees.

New Caledonian crows use sticks, twigs, or stiff pandanus leaves to probe for grubs in logs. If that approach proves unsuccessful, the crow will bend a stick, twig, or stem into a hook instead. Now the crow can snag its meal with the hook and haul it out.

Skewers

The Galápagos woodpecker finch has figured out that short sticks or cactus spines are perfect for spearing and pulling grubs from out of holes and cracks and from under the bark of trees.

Sponges

Nesting white storks, which live in Africa, Europe, and southwestern Asia, harvest a piece of wet river moss, fly it to their nest, then squeeze it out into the mouths of their chicks. It can take the diligent stork parent many trips, often on hot and dry days, to quench its little chicks' thirst.

Capuchin monkeys, long-tailed macaques, orangutans, and chimpanzees all use leaves to scoop and drink up water that collects in hard-to-reach places, like the hollows of trees. To solve this problem, the primate might crumple a handful of leaves into a ball and drop it into the water. The monkey or ape quenches its thirst by squeezing or sucking the water from this leaf sponge. If the water is beyond the monkey's or ape's reach, it will use a stick to fish out its water-soaked sponge.

The Florida harvester ant loves honey and likes to have a good store of it on hand at all times. Ants don't have buckets, jars, or even hands for collecting and transporting their beloved food. Instead, they make small pellets of sand, which they drop into a batch of honey found in a tree hollow or hive. The pellets absorb the honey, and the ants carry each sweet package home to store away for later use.

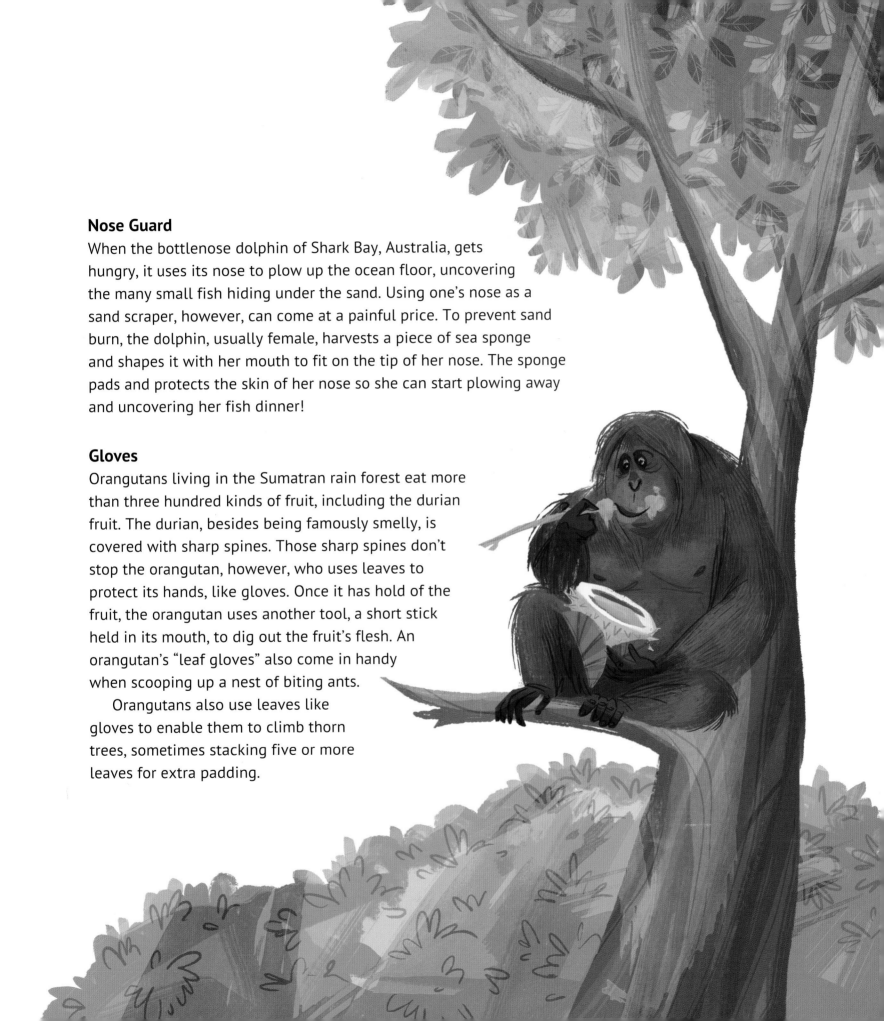

Nose Guard

When the bottlenose dolphin of Shark Bay, Australia, gets hungry, it uses its nose to plow up the ocean floor, uncovering the many small fish hiding under the sand. Using one's nose as a sand scraper, however, can come at a painful price. To prevent sand burn, the dolphin, usually female, harvests a piece of sea sponge and shapes it with her mouth to fit on the tip of her nose. The sponge pads and protects the skin of her nose so she can start plowing away and uncovering her fish dinner!

Gloves

Orangutans living in the Sumatran rain forest eat more than three hundred kinds of fruit, including the durian fruit. The durian, besides being famously smelly, is covered with sharp spines. Those sharp spines don't stop the orangutan, however, who uses leaves to protect its hands, like gloves. Once it has hold of the fruit, the orangutan uses another tool, a short stick held in its mouth, to dig out the fruit's flesh. An orangutan's "leaf gloves" also come in handy when scooping up a nest of biting ants.

Orangutans also use leaves like gloves to enable them to climb thorn trees, sometimes stacking five or more leaves for extra padding.

TOOLS FOR COMFORT

Many animals search out safe, out-of-the-way places to sleep, to hide, or to wait out bad weather. Some even take measures—using tools—to make these places extra comfortable.

Umbrellas and Hats

Like people, orangutans don't really like to get wet unless they're going for a swim. When it rains in the tropical forest, which it does a lot, an orangutan often holds a large leaf, like the leaf of a banana tree, or a bunch of leaves over its head. *Presto!*—instant umbrella. It might also hold up one of these "umbrellas" to shade itself from the sun.

An orangutan will sometimes balance a leaf on its head, like a wide-brimmed hat. Either way, it does the job!

Flyswatters

When an elephant is annoyed by a swarm of flies, it won't just stand around wishing they would buzz off. The elephant grasps a leafy branch in its trunk and shoos the flies away with that jumbo flyswatter. Orangutans do the same.

Canopy

To keep its nest and babies dry during the rainy season, and shaded during the hottest times of year, the shy, long-tailed tailorbird of southern China, southeastern Asia, and India does a bit of sewing.

The bird first uses its beak to pierce tiny holes all along the edges of a large leaf. Next it gathers spiderwebs or thin plant fibers to use as thread. Like a tailor sewing a seam, the bird takes the "thread" in its beak and, by pushing and pulling it through the holes, stitches one edge of the leaf to the other until it has made a small basket. Last, it pulls a leaf over the top of the basket and sews it into place. The nest is like a gently swinging cradle with a canopy, perfect for raising young tailorbirds in protective comfort.

Beds, Blankets, and Pillows

Almost every night, an orangutan builds itself a new sleeping nest up in a tree using sticks, twigs, and leaves. What's even more amazing is that it often hauls up extra leaves to use as a kind of blanket. But it doesn't stop there. An orangutan also bundles together leaves, moss, or other soft material on which to rest its weary head. *Ahh!* A comfy pillow!

Dolls

Orangutans have the longest childhood of any animals in the world (excluding humans!). Mother orangutans give birth about every eight years, and their young stay with them into their teen years. During this extended childhood, young orangutans learn survival and life skills by observing and imitating their mother, which would usually include watching her care for a younger sibling.

Young female orangutans in particular, in Borneo and Sumatra, have been observed taking small bundles of leaves to bed with them. They hold and cuddle these bundles through the night, as a human child might do with a doll. This behavior might very well be practice for the day they have little orangutans of their own.

Young chimpanzees engage in similar behavior, using a favorite stick instead of a leaf bundle as a doll.

. . . AND JOY

Play is a major developmental activity for humans and other animals. Play not only reduces stress and promotes social bonding; it can also provide an important form of early learning. Play is one of the best ways of figuring out and understanding how things work.

Sledding

Crows have been observed using an object such as a jar lid to slide down a snow-covered roof, just for the fun of it.

A Game of Catch

A raven will play a game of catch with itself, tossing a stick in the air and then trying to catch it.

King of the Hill

Pairs of white-necked ravens some-times play a game like King of the Hill. One raven finds higher ground and holds a piece of dung in its beak. The other charges up and attempts to snatch the dung away. If that bird succeeds, it's now "king of the hill," and the lucky holder of the dung. Yay!

Stick Tag

Common ravens love playing a game researchers call Stick Tag. A group of ravens, one of whom is holding a stick, flies into the sky. The others give chase until the stick holder lets go. As the stick falls, another raven swoops down and grabs it out of the air, taking its turn as the one to be chased.

Joyriding

Birds sometimes clutch pieces of bark in their talons for a kind of magic carpet ride on the wind's currents.

And a Proto-Tool: Ice-Skating

(While this isn't an example of true tool use, it is such a fun example of proto-tool use that it snuck into the book! A proto-tool is an object that is utilized for a purpose but is not held or manipulated; examples include a stationary boulder used as an anvil or, in this case, an iced-over lake used as a sliding surface.)

   Herds of American bison have been spotted taking running leaps onto a frozen lake. Spreading their feet for better stability, the shaggy beasts raise their tails and bellow happily, all while spinning and sliding across the lake in the bison Ice Capades!

CONCLUSION

Just like humans, many animals of the wild are confronted every day with basic needs for food, safety, shelter, comfort, or just plain feel-good fun. From all corners of this grand, glorious, sometimes dangerous world we live in, animals must overcome daily obstacles. They have learned, often through trial and error, to satisfy these needs by turning to their environment, studying it, and fashioning or devising objects into tools.

Like us, they think. They study. They consider. They try and try again until one day . . . voilà! The task before them, the goal just out of reach, the thing that they need and want the most, is now within reach. What seemed impossible is now possible, thanks to the use of a tool.

Tool use! Puzzling . . . seeing . . . studying . . . acting. From the mighty orangutan's making of a leaf glove or an umbrella-leaf hat to the small, lowly assassin bug dangling the carcass of a termite as bait, animals have come up with extremely clever ways to solve problems.

Creatures great and small, from across this beautifully fragile third planet from the sun that we call Earth, have discovered resourceful ways to take care of themselves and get the job done—by using tools.

GLOSSARY

anti-inflammatory: having properties that work to reduce swelling or inflammation

antiseptic: a substance that slows or prevents the growth of bacteria and other germs that can cause infection and disease

anvil: usually a large block of metal with a flat top on which things are struck or flattened

barbed: having sharp projections

biologist: a scientist who studies organisms

canopy: the uppermost part of a forest including the upper branches of trees

carcass: the dead body of an animal

colony: several individual organisms (usually of the same species) living close together

diplomacy: negotiations without violence

dominance: having greater power than or influence over someone or something else

fledge: to grow feathers big enough for flight

hypostome: a structure similar to a harpoon that is part of the mouth of some animals such as ticks

paralyzed: partially or totally incapable of movement

pellet: a small rounded mass of a material such as food

predator: an organism that kills and eats other organisms

prey: an organism that is hunted, killed, and eaten by other organisms

primatologist: a scientist who studies primates, an order of mammals that includes apes, monkeys, and lemurs

protein: a substance that is eaten by animals to obtain essential amino acids that they cannot make themselves

proto-tool: an object that is not handled by an animal but is still used to perform some function or type of work

tentacle: a boneless, flexible limb of some animals that is used for feeling, catching food, or moving

tool: any object, fashioned or found, that is used to do a type of work and is not a naturally occurring part of the user

tuber: a swollen part of a plant's stem or a root that is underground and stores nutrients for the plant

venomous: capable of injecting or secreting venom, which is a toxic or poisonous substance

zoologist: a scientist who studies animals, including their structures, classifications, and the ecosystems in which they live

BIBLIOGRAPHY

Books

Ackerman, Jennifer. *The Genius of Birds*. New York: Penguin, 2016.

Brown, Augustus. *Why Pandas Do Handstands and Other Curious Truths About Animals*. New York: Free Press, 2006.

Ford, Barbara. *Animals That Use Tools*. New York: Simon and Schuster, 1978.

Hansell, Mike. *Built By Animals: The Natural History of Animal Architecture*. New York: Oxford University Press, 2007.

Montgomery, Sy. *The Soul of an Octopus: A Surprising Exploration into the Wonder of Consciousness*. New York: Atria, 2015.

Mustard, Alex, and Callum Roberts. *Secrets of the Seas: A Journey into the Heart of the Oceans*. New York: Bloomsbury, 2016.

Page, George. *Inside the Animal Mind*. New York: Doubleday, 1999.

Recio, Belinda. *Inside Animal Hearts and Minds: Bears That Count, Goats That Surf, and Other True Stories of Animal Emotion and Intelligence*. New York: Skyhorse, 2017.

Sanz, Crickette Marie, Josep Call, and Christophe Boesch, eds. *Tool Use in Animals: Cognition and Ecology*. Cambridge: Cambridge University Press, 2014.

Shumaker, Robert W., Kristina R. Walkup, and Benjamin B. Beck. *Animal Tool Behavior: The Use and Manufacture of Tools by Animals*. Baltimore: Johns Hopkins University Press, 2011.

Turner, Pamela S. *Crow Smarts: Inside the Brain of the World's Brightest Bird*. Boston: Houghton Mifflin Harcourt, 2016.

Articles

Choi, Charles Q. "10 Animals That Use Tools." *Live Science*, December 14, 2009. https://www.livescience.com/9761-10-animals-tools.html.

Ford, Colin, and J.D. McKay. "Creature Feature: Boxer Crabs." Coral Morphologic website. http://coral morphologic.com/b/creature-feature-boxer-crabs.

Gray, Richard. "Bonobos Give a Glimpse Back in Time to Stone Age Man: Apes Seen Making Wooden Spears, Daggers and Stone Shovels Like Our Human Ancestors." *Daily Mail*, July 8, 2015. http://www.dailymail.co.uk/sciencetech/article-3153320/Bonobos-glimpse-time-Stone-Age-man-Apes-seen-making-wooden-spears-daggers-stone-shovels-like-human-ancestors.html.

Holdrege, Craig. "Elephantine Intelligence." *In Context* (Nature Institute newsletter), no. 5 (Spring 2001): 10–13. http://natureinstitute.org/pub/ic/ic5/elephant.htm.

Hopkin, Michael. "Hungry Monkeys Can Dig It: Capuchins in Brazil Spotted Using Tools to Unearth Food." *Nature*, December 9, 2004. http://www.nature.com/news/2004/041206/full/news041206-12.html.

Kamrani, Kambiz. "Orangutan from Borneo Photographed Using a Spear Tool to Fish." Primatology.net, April 29, 2008. https://primatology.net/2008/04/29/orangutan-photographed-using-tool-as-spear-to-fish/.

Naish, Darrin. "Tool Use in Crocodylians: Crocodiles and Alligators Use Sticks as Lures to Attract Waterbirds." Tetrapod Zoology blog, Scientific American, November 30, 2013. https://blogs.scientificamerican.com/tetrapod-zoology/tool-use-in-crocodylians-crocodiles-and-alligators-use-sticks-as-lures-to-attract-waterbirds/.

Nelson, Bryan. "15 remarkable animals that use tools." Mother Nature Network, October 28, 2009. https://www.mnn.com/earth-matters/wilderness-resources/photos/15-remarkable-animals-that-use-tools/handymen#top-desktop.

S., Kacee. "8 Facts About the Pom-Pom Crab." PADI blog, May 14, 2015. http://www2.padi.com/blog/2015/05/14/facts-about-the-pom-pom-crab/.

INDEX

To Megan, for everything
RH

For Matthew, Megan, and Benjamin
SL

First edition 2021

Library of Congress Catalog Card Number pending
ISBN 978-1-5362-0093-5

21 22 23 24 25 26 TWP 10 9 8 7 6 5 4 3 2 1

Printed in Johor Bahru, Malaysia

This book was typeset in PT Sans.
The illustrations were created digitally.

Candlewick Press
99 Dover Street
Somerville, Massachusetts 02144

www.candlewick.com